The

Birthday Book

by

ARCHER HOUSE

The Birthday Book

This product is published by Archer House Ltd.

Archer House Limited, Archer House, Dept 41,
P.O Box 59114, LONDON, England
NW2 9EU

ARCHER HOUSE

Printed in England by PJ Print

www.thebirthdaybook.com

Owner's Information

Name:

Address

Telephone:

Mobile:

Email:

Work address:

Work telephone:

Next of kin:

Reward if found:

Birth Signs

		Birthstone	Element	Key phrase
Aries The Ram	March 21 - April 19	Diamond	Fire	I am
Taurus The Bull	April 20 - May 20	Emerald	Earth	I have
Gemini The Twins	May 21 - June 21	Agate	Air	I think
Cancer The Crab	June 22 - July 22	Pearl	Water	I feel
Leo The Lion	July 23 - August 22	Ruby	Fire	I will
Virgo The Virgin	August 23 - September 22	Sapphire	Earth	I analyse
Libra The Scales	September 23 - October 22	Opal	Air	I balance
Scorpio The Scorpion	October 23 - November 21	Topaz	Water	I desire
Sagittarius The Archer	November 22 - December 21	Turquoise	Fire	I understand
Capricorn The Goat	December 22 - January 19	Garnet	Earth	I use
Aquarius The Water Bearer	January 20 - February 18	Amethyst	Air	I know
Pisces The Fishes	February 19 - March 20	Aquamarine	Water	I believe

name	1	year born	name	2	year born	name	3	year born

name	7	year born	name	8	year born	name	9	year born

name	13	year born	name	14	year born	name	15	year born

name	19	year born	name	20	year born	name	21	year born

name	25	year born	name	26	year born	name	27	year born

January

name	4	year born
....	....	
....	....	
....	....	
....	....	

name	5	year born
....	....	
....	....	
....	....	
....	....	

name	6	year born
....	....	
....	....	
....	....	
....	....	

name	10	year born
....	....	
....	....	
....	....	
....	....	

name	11	year born
....	....	
....	....	
....	....	
....	....	

name	12	year born
....	....	
....	....	
....	....	
....	....	

name	16	year born
....	....	
....	....	
....	....	
....	....	

name	17	year born
....	....	
....	....	
....	....	
....	....	

name	18	year born
....	....	
....	....	
....	....	
....	....	

name	22	year born
....	....	
....	....	
....	....	
....	....	

name	23	year born
....	....	
....	....	
....	....	
....	....	

name	24	year born
....	....	
....	....	
....	....	
....	....	

name	28	year born
....	....	
....	....	
....	....	
....	....	

name	29	year born
....	....	
....	....	
....	....	
....	....	

name	30	year born
....	....	
....	....	
....	....	
....	....	

name	31	year born
....	....	
....	....	

name		year born
....	....	
....	....	

name	1	year born	name	2	year born	name	3	year born

name	7	year born	name	8	year born	name	9	year born

name	13	year born	name	14	year born	name	15	year born

name	19	year born	name	20	year born	name	21	year born

name	25	year born	name	26	year born	name	27	year born

February

name	4	year born	name	5	year born	name	6	year born

name	10	year born	name	11	year born	name	12	year born

name	16	year born	name	17	year born	name	18	year born

name	22	year born	name	23	year born	name	24	year born

name	28	year born	name	29	year born

name	1	year born	name	2	year born	name	3	year born

name	7	year born	name	8	year born	name	9	year born

name	13	year born	name	14	year born	name	15	year born

name	19	year born	name	20	year born	name	21	year born

name	25	year born	name	26	year born	name	27	year born

March

name	4	year born

name	5	year born

name	6	year born

name	10	year born

name	11	year born

name	12	year born

name	16	year born

name	17	year born

name	18	year born

name	22	year born

name	23	year born

name	24	year born

name	28	year born

name	29	year born

name	30	year born

name	31	year born

name		year born

name	1	year born	name	2	year born	name	3	year born

name	7	year born	name	8	year born	name	9	year born

name	13	year born	name	14	year born	name	15	year born

name	19	year born	name	20	year born	name	21	year born

name	25	year born	name	26	year born	name	27	year born

April

name	4	year born	name	5	year born	name	6	year born

name	10	year born	name	11	year born	name	12	year born

name	16	year born	name	17	year born	name	18	year born

name	22	year born	name	23	year born	name	24	year born

name	28	year born	name	29	year born	name	30	year born

name	1	year born	name	2	year born	name	3	year born

name	7	year born	name	8	year born	name	9	year born

name	13	year born	name	14	year born	name	15	year born

name	19	year born	name	20	year born	name	21	year born

name	25	year born	name	26	year born	name	27	year born

May

name	4	year born
....		
....		
....		
....		

name	5	year born
....		
....		
....		
....		

name	6	year born
....		
....		
....		
....		

name	10	year born
....		
....		
....		
....		

name	11	year born
....		
....		
....		
....		

name	12	year born
....		
....		
....		
....		

name	16	year born
....		
....		
....		
....		

name	17	year born
....		
....		
....		
....		

name	18	year born
....		
....		
....		
....		

name	22	year born
....		
....		
....		
....		

name	23	year born
....		
....		
....		
....		

name	24	year born
....		
....		
....		
....		

name	28	year born
....		
....		
....		
....		

name	29	year born
....		
....		
....		
....		

name	30	year born
....		
....		
....		
....		

name	31	year born
....		
....		

name		year born
....		
....		

name	1	year born	name	2	year born	name	3	year born

name	7	year born	name	8	year born	name	9	year born

name	13	year born	name	14	year born	name	15	year born

name	19	year born	name	20	year born	name	21	year born

name	25	year born	name	26	year born	name	27	year born

June

name	4	year born	name	5	year born	name	6	year born

name	10	year born	name	11	year born	name	12	year born

name	16	year born	name	17	year born	name	18	year born

name	22	year born	name	23	year born	name	24	year born

name	28	year born	name	29	year born	name	30	year born

name	1	year born	name	2	year born	name	3	year born

name	7	year born	name	8	year born	name	9	year born

name	13	year born	name	14	year born	name	15	year born

name	19	year born	name	20	year born	name	21	year born

name	25	year born	name	26	year born	name	27	year born

July

name	4	year born

name	5	year born

name	6	year born

name	10	year born

name	11	year born

name	12	year born

name	16	year born

name	17	year born

name	18	year born

name	22	year born

name	23	year born

name	24	year born

name	28	year born

name	29	year born

name	30	year born

name	31	year born

name		year born

name		year born	name		year born	name		year born
	1			*2*			*3*	

name		year born	name		year born	name		year born
	7			*8*			*9*	

name		year born	name		year born	name		year born
	13			*14*			*15*	

name		year born	name		year born	name		year born
	19			*20*			*21*	

name		year born	name		year born	name		year born
	25			*26*			*27*	

August

name	4	year born

name	5	year born

name	6	year born

name	10	year born

name	11	year born

name	12	year born

name	16	year born

name	17	year born

name	18	year born

name	22	year born

name	23	year born

name	24	year born

name	28	year born

name	29	year born

name	30	year born

name	31	year born

name		year born

name	1	year born	name	2	year born	name	3	year born

name	7	year born	name	8	year born	name	9	year born

name	13	year born	name	14	year born	name	15	year born

name	19	year born	name	20	year born	name	21	year born

name	25	year born	name	26	year born	name	27	year born

September

name	4	year born	name	5	year born	name	6	year born

name	10	year born	name	11	year born	name	12	year born

name	16	year born	name	17	year born	name	18	year born

name	22	year born	name	23	year born	name	24	year born

name	28	year born	name	29	year born	name	30	year born

name	1	year born	name	2	year born	name	3	year born

name	7	year born	name	8	year born	name	9	year born

name	13	year born	name	14	year born	name	15	year born

name	19	year born	name	20	year born	name	21	year born

name	25	year born	name	26	year born	name	27	year born

October

name	4	year born

name	5	year born

name	6	year born

name	10	year born

name	11	year born

name	12	year born

name	16	year born

name	17	year born

name	18	year born

name	22	year born

name	23	year born

name	24	year born

name	28	year born

name	29	year born

name	30	year born

name	31	year born

name		year born

name	1	year born	name	2	year born	name	3	year born

name	7	year born	name	8	year born	name	9	year born

name	13	year born	name	14	year born	name	15	year born

name	19	year born	name	20	year born	name	21	year born

name	25	year born	name	26	year born	name	27	year born

November

name	4	year born

name	5	year born

name	6	year born

name	10	year born

name	11	year born

name	12	year born

name	16	year born

name	17	year born

name	18	year born

name	22	year born

name	23	year born

name	24	year born

name	28	year born

name	29	year born

name	30	year born

name 1 year born	name 2 year born	name 3 year born

name 7 year born	name 8 year born	name 9 year born

name 13 year born	name 14 year born	name 15 year born

name 19 year born	name 20 year born	name 21 year born

name 25 year born	name 26 year born	name 27 year born

December

name	4	year born

name	5	year born

name	6	year born

name	10	year born

name	11	year born

name	12	year born

name	16	year born

name	17	year born

name	18	year born

name	22	year born

name	23	year born

name	24	year born

name	28	year born

name	29	year born

name	30	year born

name	31	year born

name		year born

Notes

Notes

Notes

Notes

Should you wish to order further copies of this publication

Please contact us:-

i nfo@thebirthdaybook.com

or

www.thebirthdaybook.com

or

*Archer House Limited, Archer House, Dept 41,
P.O Box 59114, LONDON, England NW2 9EU*

or

+44 (0)20 8902 6403

Corporate and licensee enquiries are always welcomed

Lightning Source UK Ltd.
Milton Keynes UK
UKHW011834051021
391739UK00001B/94